Created & illustration
Rejane Dal Bello

Words & story
Jayshree Viswanathan

Medical strategy
Stefan Liute

Dr. Giraffe

Once there was
a little giraffe

Who wished she
had a matching half.

Instead of halves that made a whole

Left
right

and

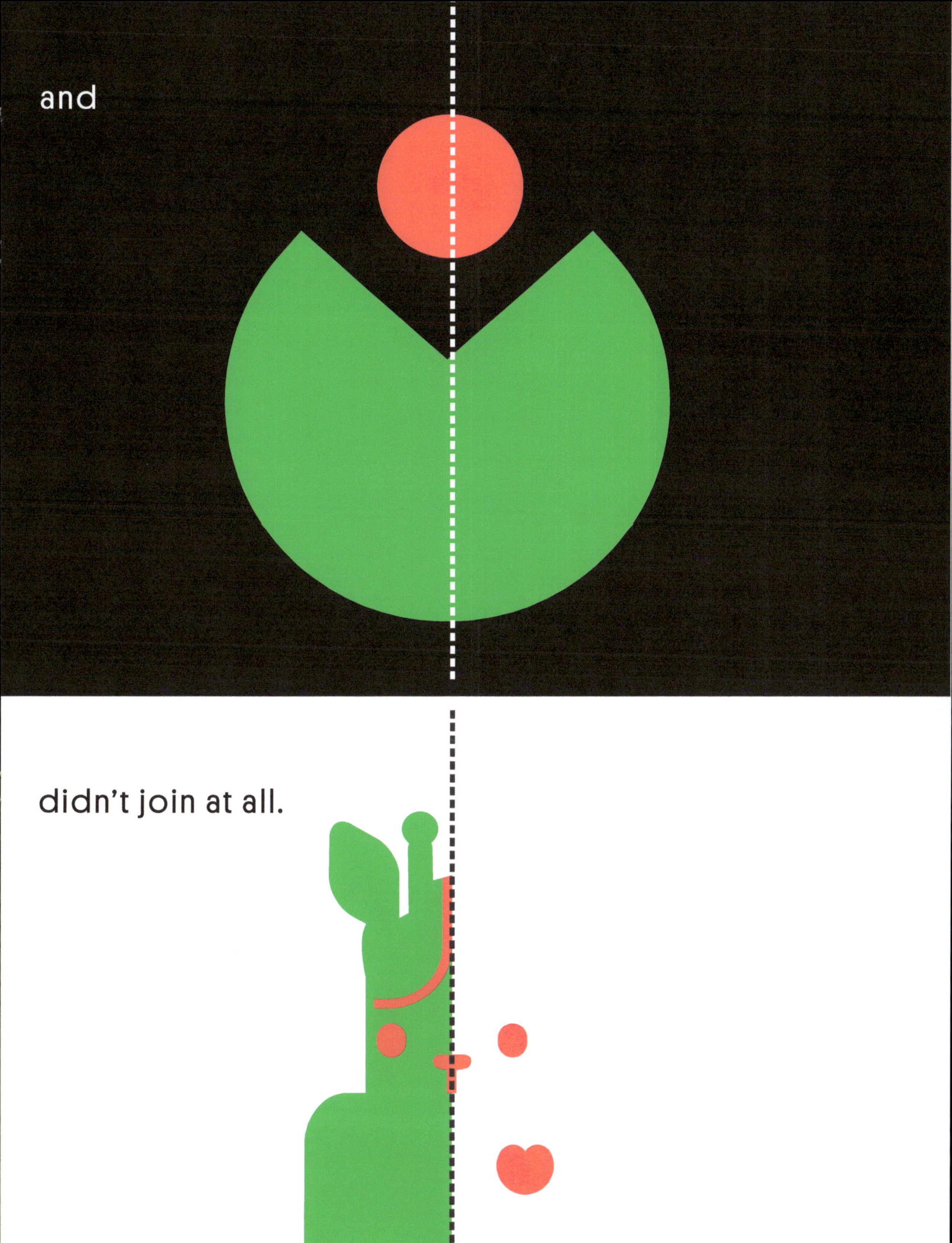

Smiling half
a smile

Speaking in half sounds

She ate from
a dinner plate

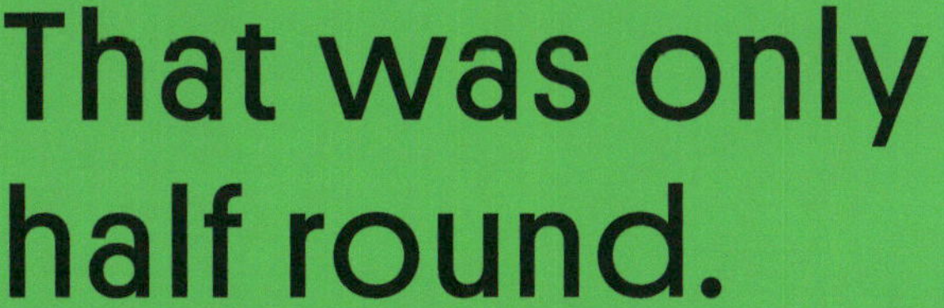
That was only
half round.

She tried on
new halves

But they didn't
fit

None of them
was right,

Not even
a bit.

Some were
too silly

Some were too sticky

Others
were just
a little too
zippy.

One was
too messy

Another
kept tickling!

Yet another
had glasses,

that
wouldn't
stop
slipping.

She tried to
be invisible

But people
still stared

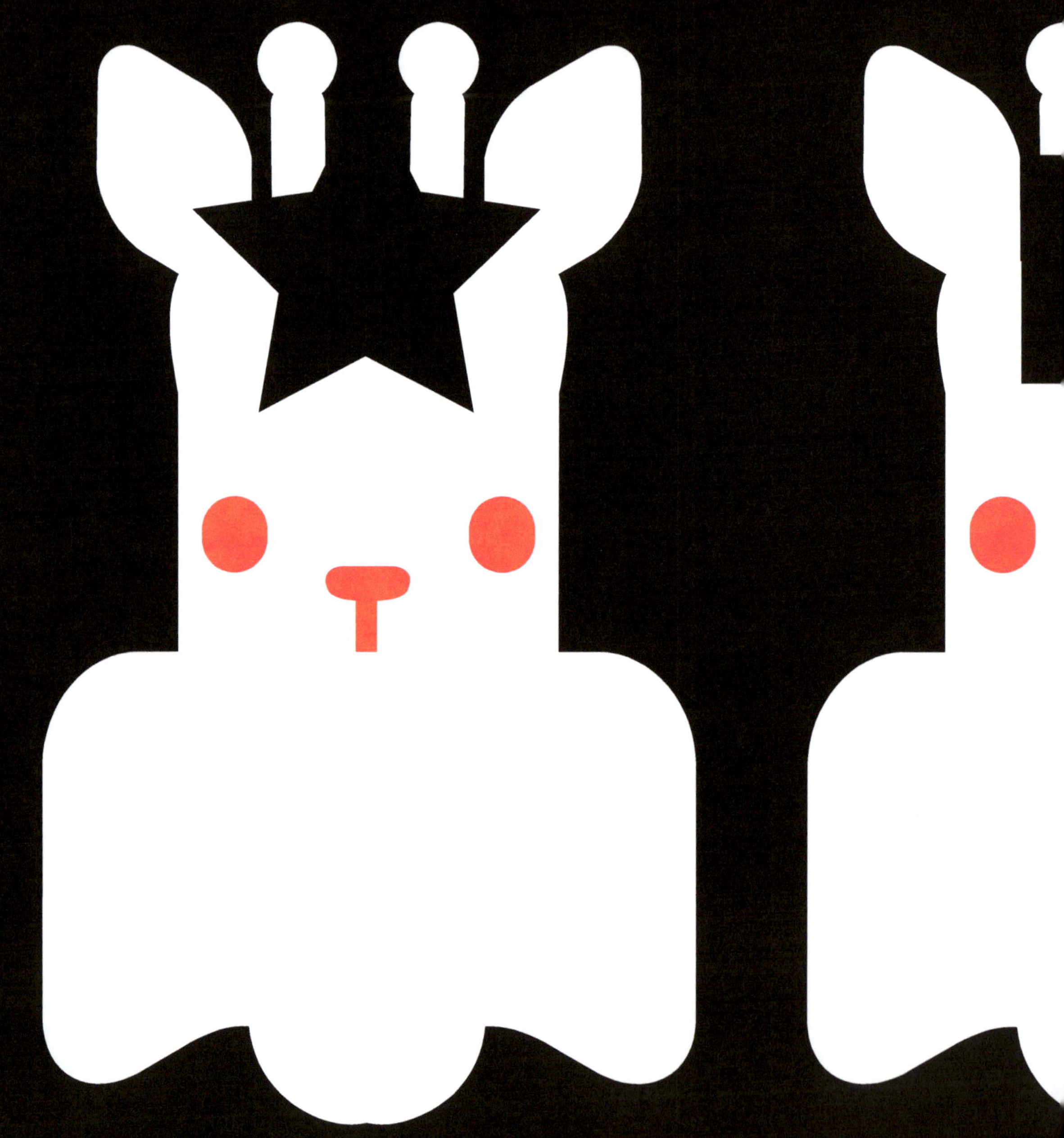

From friends she felt
so different

Her little heart despaired.

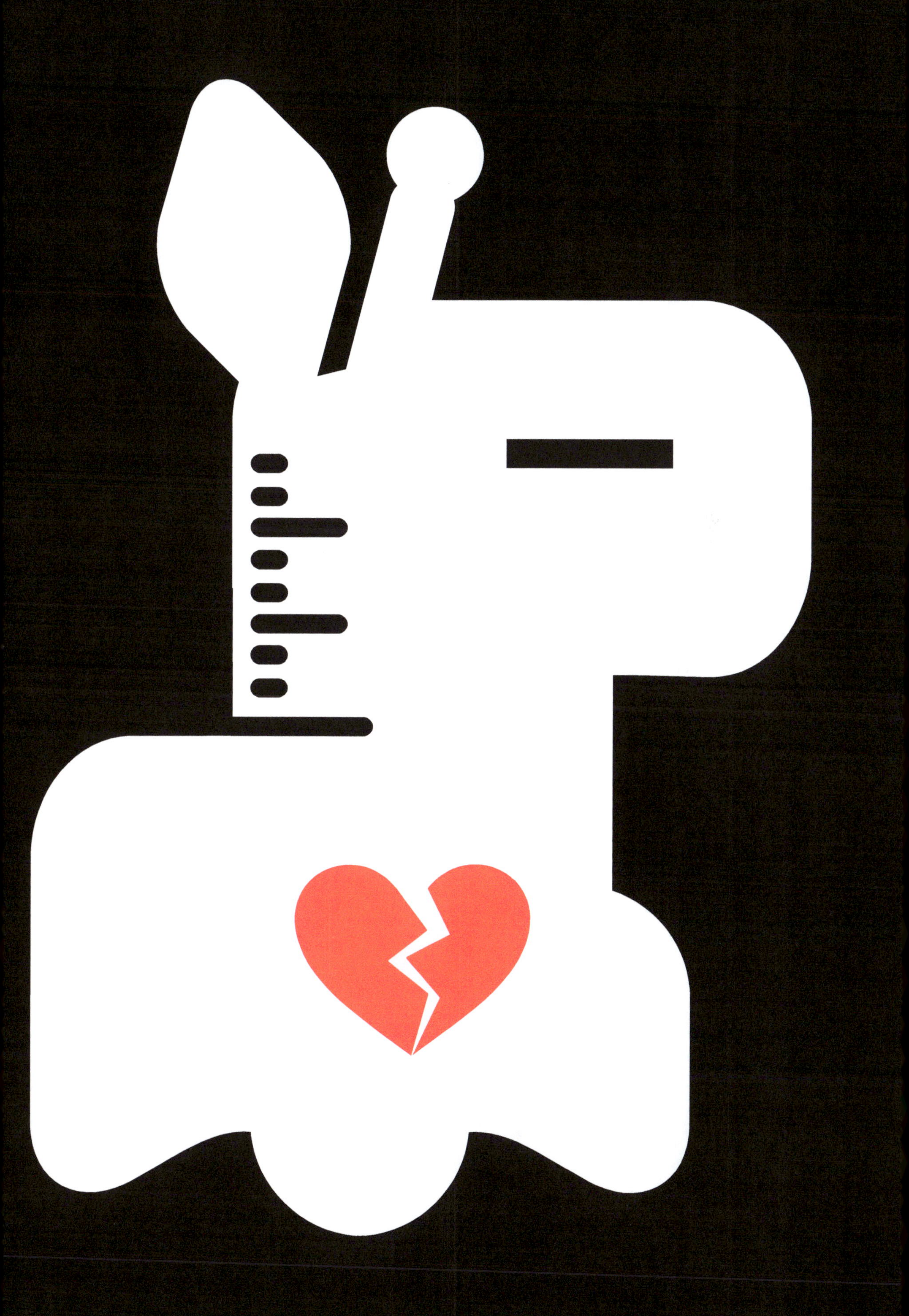

Then all
at once,

Our giraffe
found a half

That was just
right for her

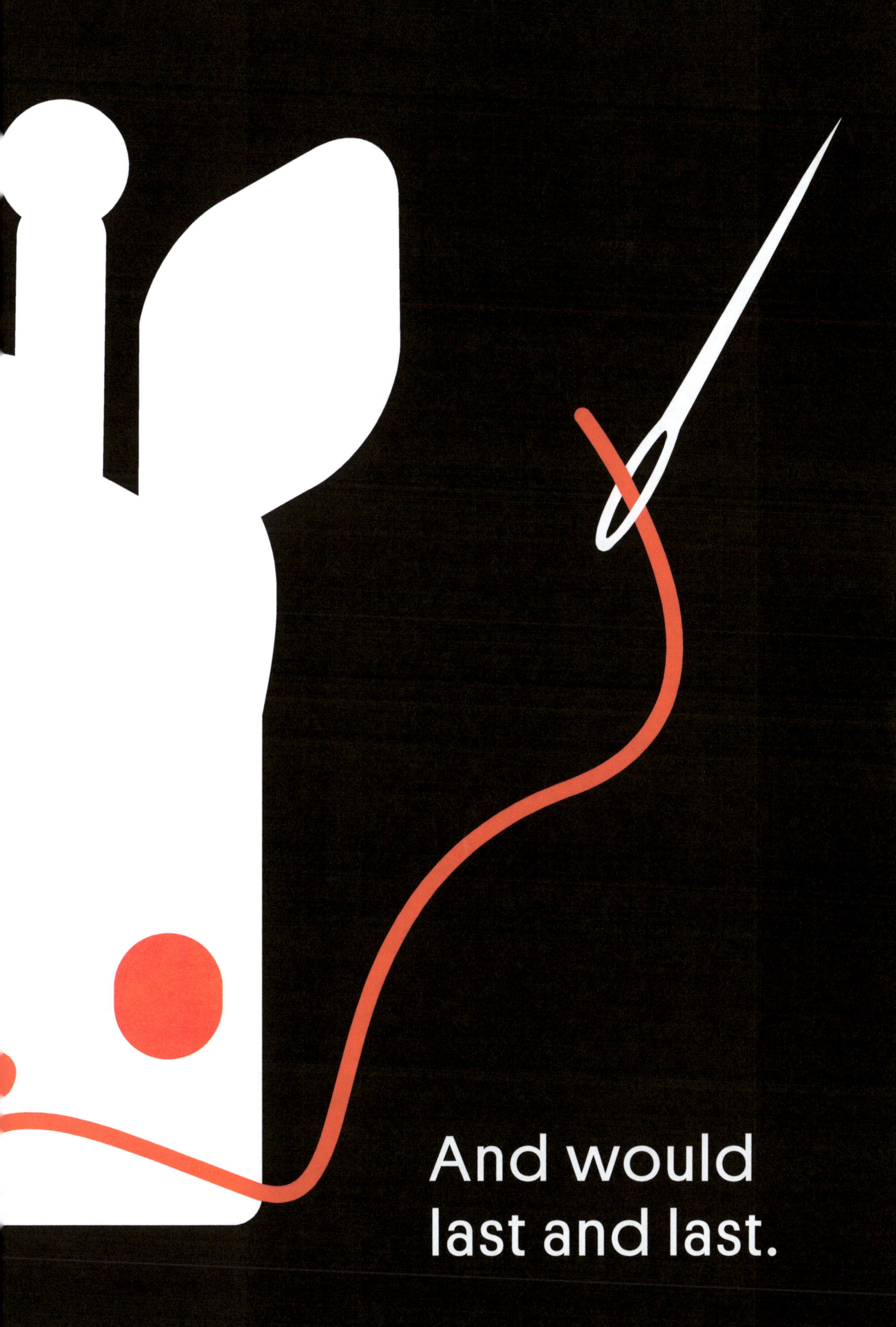
And would
last and last.

'Be patient'
said Mama

"You have
to go steady,

And wait
and wait

Until your
half's finally
ready."

So that's
what she did

Until, she
at last

Came face
to face

With her own
matching half.

But wait,
what was
this?

Though
matching
outside

She still
felt quite
different

And half-half
inside.

She could still
only speak

In half words
or less

And her mouth
would not smile

Though she
tried her best.

'Be patient'
said Mama

As she said before,
'In order to match

You must first
wait some more.'

So to pass
the time

She practised
her sounds

mm

Like 'M' for Mama
Until she was proud.

Sounds joined into words

And her joined up speaking

And words joined into phrases

Soon earned Mama's praises.

To pass some
more time

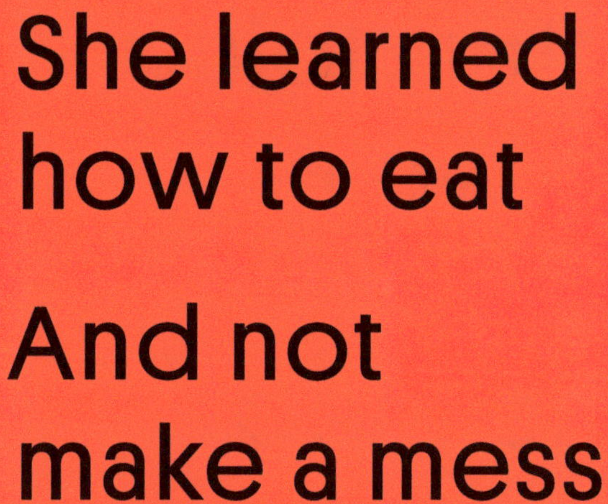

She learned
how to eat

And not
make a mess

So mealtimes
were neat.

After doing
so well

She tried
one more
thing:

She wanted
to smile

To make
Mama's
heart sing.

Slowly,
slowly

Up and
down,

Her lips
learned to
curve

Until she
forgot how
to frown.

Then at
long last,

Came the
day she'd
awaited

she was no
longer half

But fully
completed

Not only on the
outside

But also
within

And Little Giraffe
never felt

Half-half again.

The end.

Created, illustrated & designed by

Rejane Dal Bello is an award-winning graphic designer and
illustrator, with a great range of iconic design case studies
to her name. Her design house Studio Rejane Dal Bello creates
branding and visual identities for national and international
clients, especially focusing on the corporate, arts and culture and
non-profit sectors.
rejanedalbello.com

Words & story by

Jayshree Viswanathan is a copywriter and poetry lover, who crafts
words and ideas for commercial brands. She has also collaborated
with arts organisations, small businesses, and film production
houses, helping them find the best words for their creative
ventures. A lifelong dreamer, she's a firm believer
in the power of creativity, especially for good.
jayshreeviswanathan.com

Medical strategy by

Stefan Liute is the co-founder and strategy director of Storience, a
branding agency that helps brands create positive social impact.
He also co-founded digital agency Grapefruit, creating digital user
experiences to make people's lives easier. A former medical doctor
turned strategist, he thinks business, technology, and humanity can
find a way to co-exist.
storience.com

Supported by

Marjan van Mourik and Paz Holandesa Hospital, a
non-profit children's hospital in Arequipa, Peru. Branding
for Paz Holandesa was sponsored by Studio Rejane Dal Bello,
and is still ongoing. As hospital founder, Marjan is devoted
to this unique design collaboration and continues to inspire and
support its development.
pazholandesa.com

We cannot avoid illness, but we can ease it by making disease less abstract and more human. The Dr Giraffe series was created to inform and comfort children afflicted with childhood diseases, from common ailments to rare conditions. Through his comforting presence and a simple story, Dr Giraffe helps young patients and their parents understand what the body is going through and what to expect. Our ambition is to make Dr Giraffe a global ambassador for childhood disease, explaining and offering comfort for illnesses and ailments all around the world. To make this ambition a reality, we need your help to continue.

Our collection so far

— Mr. Dot: chicken pox
— Half-half: cleft palate and lip
— Huff, puff: asthma
— Land of the Big: leukaemia

Our shop
drgiraffe.com

Supporting Dr Giraffe

If you are interested in helping us grow the Dr Giraffe series with a donation or supporting our project by becoming a member, please contact:

drgiraffe.com/support-us

Chicken pox

Cleft palate

Asthma

Leukaemia